Indigo Dreams Revisited

W0013915

Ronnie Goodyer

Indigo Dreams Publishing

This edition first published in Great Britain 2010 by:
Indigo Dreams Publishing
132 Hinckley Road
Stoney Stanton
Leicestershire
LE9 4LN

www.indigodreams.co.uk

'Indigo Dreams' first published in original form by Bluechrome 2003
ISBN 0-9543796-2-4
Revised and updated 2010

ISBN 978-1-907401-28-2

British Library Cataloguing in Publication Data. A CIP record for this
book can be obtained from the British Library.

Cover, all sketches/digital images and manipulations by Ronnie Goodyer

Designed and typeset in Garamond by Indigo Dreams Publishing

Printed and bound in Great Britain by Imprint Academic, Exeter

Acknowledgements

Many of the poems in this collection have appeared in poetry magazines, including, Aireings, Aesthetica, Aspire, Black Mountain Review, Coffee House Poetry, The Coffee House, The Dawntreader, Dial 174, Eclipse, Envoi, Harlequin, iota, The Journal, Konfluence, Moonstone, Poetry Cornwall, Poetry Monthly, Pulsar, The New Writer, Poetry Nottingham International, Psychopoetica, Purple Patch, Poet Tree, Solo Survivors, Rain Dog, Reach Poetry, Sarasvati and Voice and Verse.

Previous collections:
Within The Silence - ISBN 1-900824-17-5 2001 (With Michael K Moore)
Indigo Dreams – ISBN 0-9543796-2-4   2003
Lizard Reality – ISBN 0-9543796-8-3   2004
New Words From An Old Hat – ISBN 978-0-9553589-0-6   2006
The Way Of The Dance – ISBN 978-0-9553589-6-8   2009

Dedication

To all who have journeyed with me,
all I am meeting here for the first time,
Dawn who is making the journey special,
and Darren and Hannah who have always been there.

Indigo Dreams

Switch on the moonlight,
wrap yourself in clouds,
share one common breath,
sleep in indigo dreams.

CONTENTS

Indigo Dreams Revisited

THAT LOVING FEELING

"abstruse perfection, someone said –
with mind alive and body yawning."

In St. Keverne

I've put the dream-catcher where it can trap the night's fear
and turn it to beauty with the fantasy of our daydreams;

I've put the bamboo chimes where they can sway in the sea- breeze
and send music in gentle tones to the garden beyond;

I've put the purple and gold shawl over the old rocker by the hearth
where you can be tempted to put a demanding day on hold;

I've put our old battered lamp in the room's far corner
where its familiar light can rest easy on our eyes;

I've put driftwood in the stone by the summer fireplace
where thoughts can turn to beach-combed serenity;

I've put the beads and trinkets from Thassos in obscure corners
where blue skies and retsina days can cover the blankness of space;

I've put crystals in many windows where they can follow the sun
and paint rainbow prisms until the west windows fill with pink;

I've put the beautiful candles in safe places where colour can scent
and its light diffuse on the picked border flowers held in terracotta;

I've put your rickety favourite chair by the hedge near the front door
where the Lizard wind is eased, the sun sits and the kitchen is near;

I've put bohemian days and nights far from arcadia
and spread skeletons of life on the carpet at your feet;

I've put arms out to catch you, my faith in love exposed
and wake each day to find I'm still in Elysian fields.

She Clicks The Keys

Her world is mostly in her head
as she clicks the keys of my morning.
Cold toast and kisses, body fed,
her world is mostly in her head –
abstruse perfection, someone said –
with mind alive and body yawning.
Her world is mostly in her head
as she clicks the keys of my morning.

The Right Words To Say

I was once advised not to use 'beautiful'
just write as clearly as you see the vision;
add shimmers of verbs darkened with reason;
bring through a forest's enchantment
and let it glow like a kingfisher in moist air;
use truth, like a tear on the face of a friend
and the strength of a butterfly in a rogue wind;
first love when your heart is screaming
and sunlight, sleeping in pools of golden leaves;
choose the blue hills that mix with stars
and add the towering yellows of autumn.

This is the advice I was given
but I'll still call you beautiful
as I search for the right words to say.

Let's not go out on this winter day

Let's not go out on this winter day,
the wind is shouting at the walls,
the fire won't take that long to catch,
the softness of the sofa calls.

Let's not go out on this winter day,
let's both hold still and think of ways
to travel worlds inside our heads,
refuse the places winter stays.

Let's walk through books, let's walk through poems,
visit Fern Hill and Dover Beach;
to Yeats' Lake Isle of lnnisfree,
Frost's America, Homer's Greece.

Let's drink too much and let's laugh too loud
let's find what sheer indulgence brings!
Let's clink our glasses while we can
and catch each other's hiccupping!

Then let our music resound from rooms,
as we struggle to sing as one,
Strawberry Fields, Forever Young,
Redemption Song, Here Comes The Sun.

Let's not go out on this winter day
but well before the flames expire,
let's sink into each others arms,
make love before our winter fire.

Celtic Lady

And here, Celtic Lady, I give you the morning,
the breath of Gaia, both virgin and true.
I know you will live it
and that's why I give it;
reward you can call for something that's due,
for being special, for just being you.

And here, Celtic Lady, I give you a legend,
land of your fathers that's cast out in stone.
The dolmen to seal it
and I know you feel it;
in ancient history your future is sown,
embrace the free wind, because it's your own.

And here, Celtic Lady, I give you earth's crystals,
that formed in this world when our eyes couldn't see.
I know you will wear them
and know you will share them;
I give them to you in the hope you will be
lovely as the princess who gave them to me.

And here, Celtic Lady, I give you the evening,
to reflect on a day with spirit and smiles.
The care we have taken
for love to awaken,
as gentle as nature, precious as a child;
I'm happy my life is with you for a while.

An August Tuesday, Thassos

Dust high from the tyre-track
powdered your yellow vest,
the one with the low-cut sides
where you could see your breasts.

Cicadas, moon, firefly night of breaking nature.
You were complaining of not feeling right,
because the bright honeyed day
had left your face too flushed.

We'd got about a thousand lost hours
wrapped on that taverna table
and in a woozy three-way hug with Kostas
Thassos roared in small voices,
Thassos whispered in hurricane laughs
and ice multiplied to glass d
                         r
                        o
                            p-lets.

We kissed in the grip of Greece;
we lay on the sand before dawn
and God watched the sunrise with us.
Later, we made love to an island.

Iroquois

You walk to the point of his kill,
guided by a bloody trail.
He has hung branches with guts,
strewn life organs on the path.
Perhaps your stomach churns in the sun.
Maybe you are troubled by flies
as you shake your hair,
your black hair,
over the biting cloud
swarming over the opened trophy.

Don't put on your face for me,
lady of the trees and sky;
don't pound the grain or sear the flesh.
Just let me feel the spiritual essence
and grant me the honour of your touch.
If you will allow love through warm hands,
I will thread beads into your hair,
remove your embroidered cloths and quills,
lie naked with you beside the river
and trace the moon-patterns on your skin.

Knowing....

He sat opposite her at the table.
He didn't speak but she noticed his eyes.
Ink-blue.
As they slowly drained to white,
ectoplasm bubbles fell from his closed mouth,
forming two words on the cloth:

Marry Me.

The bubbles disappeared as his mouth opened.
'Ssssh...' she smiled, 'no need to speak,
of course I will.'

Winter Visitor

After a long journey,
you arrived in my Devon winter
and we talked through Dartmoor's edge,
losing our words over Longash Hill
and our footsteps to old tracks,
wandering in the silence of history.

Breathing air of cold sweetness,
we threw patterns of laughter
that echoed back from the tors,
providing us with company,
hidden voices from high places,
forgetting we were beautiful losers.

A few days later you'd gone,
leaving the picture of boulder-green,
leaving the old track-way of reminiscence.
You'd returned to the retreat,
the sacred turf of your holy woods
and to another Celtic welcome.

After a long journey,
you wrote to say you missed me,
the companionship of another survivor
in the wilderness home of moorland.
Your letter poured warm words from the page,
reminding me of the glory summer to come.

Dunnabridge Revisited

Late July, leaning on the wooden gate,
I thought of you in your far celtic land
and how that first twist of the knife saw fate
so determined that it would lend a hand.
Fresh sunlight and the sanctity of wood,
grass heavy with birthing seed at my feet,
brought back strong memories of days we would
cross over old Dunnabridge Pound and meet.
Sometimes, like children, we'd blow on ripe grass,
or just lie in the flowering meadow,
noticing how quickly long days seemed to pass
until called home by the sun's long shadow.

Here today I'm left with longing and smiles,
thinking of you across the flying miles.

At Plymouth Barbican

Both hot,
both drinking cold cider,
apple-kisses in cushioned sun
on the flagstones and the
cobbles.

Still boats,
lifeless on the flat sea,
us not talking, just smiling,
gravity's heat,
warm love.

Hannah's Got A New Flat.

I stood in mud to watch her,
more holding on than riding
and looking so terrified in what she said was fun.

I heard her in the choir,
more sneakily sniggering than singing
and playing the recorder
in that wonderfully dodgy way.

I drank with her in her under-age,
more laughing together than drinking
and perhaps she preferred her boyfriend
in the fun of a Friday night.

I send birthday and Christmas in the post now,
more missing her than presents
and remembering paper-wrapped mornings
in the permanence of childhood.

Hannah's got a new flat.
I hear she's living with friends,
more happy home than security
and so handy for work and shops
in the unfolding of her new life.

Hannah's got a new flat.
She hasn't asked me to see it yet.

But she will……..

                                    when she's ready.

WHEN THE CANDLE DIES

"by the hospital
family leaving the ward
sun's rays burst through clouds"

That's All

It is one soft night.
With friends outside the country pub,
talking over the day, it's people.

Then who should walk by,
who should walk by after all these years ?
You, with your gypsy smile.

Memories in flood at your face,
you don't know how long or how far,
just that you must leave tomorrow.

We share seeds that may sow
and when we return, the sky's full of moon,
there's a wishing fountain I'd missed.

We seal with a kiss and you go.
Drinking to the darkness, a question –
'Why didn't she stay?'

I look to the rising fields,
islands on the bare geography.
Silence.

Some nights I drink with friends.
Some nights I drink too much.
Some nights, lately, I think of you.

But it's just a country pub thing,
that's all,
really,
that's all.................

Looking On

He stood back to admire;
the wood blocks exactly as he'd envisaged,
mitred corners seemingly growing from the walls,
no fuss, no smell, no slip.
Even the one careless mistake undetectable.
He just needed to sweep up,
put the bits in the bag,
clean the tools.

She thought she saw a light,
a silver light, sparkling over the wood.
And music, slow and melodious,
with perhaps the shadow of two people,
moving in the rhythmic moment,
as they used to before the rain set in,
before tears fell on the song,
before they danced apart.

Pantoum – The Gwynedd

Please, empty my soul – bring a hearse to clear
the life and the loves of this old house today.
Married life treasures and some twenty years,
rooms haunted with laughter of children who played.

The life and the loves of this old house today,
a family once grew here, now can you believe?
Rooms haunted with laughter of children who played,
they no longer chip paintwork or wood as they leave.

A family once grew here, now can you believe?
Faces still haunt in the bleak red wine haze.
They no longer chip paintwork or wood as they leave,
rooms may be empty but voices remain.

Faces still haunt in the bleak red wine haze
and these long summer seasons now freeze in the cold.
Rooms may be empty but voices remain
in the echoing house where I planned to grow old.

And these long summer seasons now freeze in the cold,
reflections from hallways that show just one face
in the echoing house where I planned to grow old,
changed now from a home to a vast unknown place.

Reflections from hallways that show just one face,
married life treasures and some twenty years,
changed now from a home to a vast unknown place,
please, empty my soul – bring a hearse to clear.

Spring Seeds

Early spring you took me back unknown miles
to the distant wilderness where rhymes lingered
and, swaying, burnt in your rustic garden.
I was unseasoned until your peppercorn stardust
blew a rainbow between my waiting ears.
We held gloves in glowing amber.
Night-time wrapped itself up in bulb petals
that slowly grew as we held it in our charms.
At dawn you'd gone and I missed you
like a bus that never came.

Middle spring you returned with peaches and hugs
and led me to your cliff-top cavern,
where we climbed in timeless nature.
We lay on the verges beneath outstretched trees
staring upwards to oblivion creeks
and played hide and seek with kisses and fresh cherries.
We stumbled beside ourselves on cobbled streets,
on bright lantern days and crumpled nights.
We swallowed hope with saltwater booze.
In the whisking of the Cornwall tides,
out tumbled all the cardboard fish,
left to suffocate on your once-moist lips.

Late spring you disappeared like the park squirrels.
I slept under a storm in lie-lined sheets,
silence haunting the wires above,
where the love potion dripped and dappled my dreams.
I drifted downstream into a sandalwood summer,
floating musty miles of moth-eaten memories,
sad to record that the spring seeds we planted
failed to grow into trees.

Paper-wrapped Prayer

May these greasy onion rings
become my lost salvation,
brought from the town's dark corner
in paper-wrapped love for me;

may this lone battered sausage
hold hunger in the cupboard
and crystal-encrusted chips
drown the sound of my stomach;

may alcoholic apple be the reason
for my fixed, lonely, pointless, smuggy grin;
May hogwash, babble TV
be killed by my black zapper

and thirty year old music
fight the vinyl life scratches;
let the world of my world,
in dog-snoring marrow-boned night,
say my time is yet to come.

Way Too Blue

If the advice had been there, Nick,
the green-fingered musicians would have made sure
you planted well.

Your fruit tree would have blossomed, rather than
shine briefly, each of five leaves fracture then fall.

A troubled cure for a troubled mind?
So why were you gathering the fog
whilst opening eyes?

Beautiful melancholy and way too blue,
thanks, Nick, for the strand of pain,
for the vision and the mystic. And yes -
death is the time of no reply

for nick drake

Haiku For My Mother

a telephone call
silence throughout the garden
roses held tightly

by the hospital
family leaving the ward
sun's rays burst through clouds

raindrops on marble
flowers in a metal vase
petals brush her name

anniversary
new buds on the old tree stump
weeds cleared from gravel

Lonely

The rain comes in, hits on your tears,
night-time dreams add weight to your fears;
your golden path left un-trodden,
times together just forgotten;
others escape, step out of the mess,
leave you to sink when you've done your best;
always with others whenever they sigh,
always alone when it's your turn to cry;
your head knows what being wanted would bring
but your smile's ignored, drifts off on the wind;
spice from the east and food from the south
just taste as one, choke up in your mouth;
you put on a face so no-one can tell
from the outside if you're sick or you're well;
see others' love, know you once felt it,
try not to cry, know you can't help it;
see happiness and know you can't take it,
the more that they try, the more you just fake it;

and when you cross over thinking 'now God will own me,'
will they think, maybe, sometimes, you were lonely?

At Peace At Last (Bright Moon)

Please don't worry little child,
the bright moon doesn't make a bright world
but its perfect circle can give you a perfect night.

Take a cloud's comfort little child
and sail on to another dream;
all your tears have dried on the wind now.

Keep your thoughts easy little child,
and picture your silhouette against the bright moon,
smiling as one with the rainbow - at peace at last.

(on the early death of a friend's child)

In The Garden

The stricken rose hid her colour-blood
as we walked on magnolia white
to the kissing-gate in the abandoned hedge.
Shoes were strewn by summer fruit
and the distrust flowed in scents,
differences signified in days of fire.

The old memories a wooden pretence,
sparking the ash of old feeling
and crackling with resisted blame.
We ran from the embarrassed flame
as lichen covered the mistletoe clump
and our names were missing from the bark.

You wanted to scream in the rockery blockage
as the stream stagnated with whirligig-choke
and the pathway closed, later falling.
Star-shaped back on the summer lawn
the newly born air frilled with mockery
and was alive with weeds in seed, polluting the dawn.

Your discarded clothes were now sky-rags,
dirty washing blowing free for all,
as nature avoided her own eye
and the stricken rose hid her colour-blood.

For Whom The Bell Tolls

Walking on through the blizzard, leading the twenty, the few;
scarves and hats and blinded eyes, headlong into the wind.
Three fields of waist-high snow, the few
find themselves on flattened ground.

The snow is brushed from the bell
Christ's bell - by the ransacked church.
'This bell will toll through snow' he said,
'to unite the slaughtered millions,
to resound again in the hearts of those
who lost their lives but not their faith.

And-China freezes. Indonesia, the Philippines.
'Hot coals in their eyes but they still saw;
prison bars for freedom but they still ran;
resurrection through our unification.'
1552. St Francis Xavier.
Four years dead, his body a natural colour.
1591. St John of the Cross.
Nine months dead, his blood flowing when cut.

'They are coming, Andrei, across the fields, in our tracks.'
'Then let us die like saints, let's see our birth of heaven.'
And the soldiers were called onward, their only intention to kill,
drawn by a choir of voices and the music of a muted bell.

Mary, One Morning

Mary had slept under a storm last night
and morning found her in the tubular kitchen.
She played with the drowning cereal residue,
deliberately ignored the expectant dog
and picked up the forgotten homework book.

In her spare-room and junk-room studio
she felt the complete, blank plainness of depression.
Her canvas creation, under her rain-clean stare,
became pointless pigment suspended in liquid.
Under her kick it fell top-side down to the floor
just like the buttered toast had earlier.

Mary, one morning, left a note behind.
Mary, one morning, picked up her well-travelled bags
walked out into the breeze of a wanton summer,
towards the only man she'd had an affair with,
knowing the path from home was dangerous,
hoping bohemia was safety of a kind.

WAR IN OUR TIME

"The mothers ask what kind of world
their children will grow up in
and protectively cradle them close."

witnessing the birth of peace on earth   rg

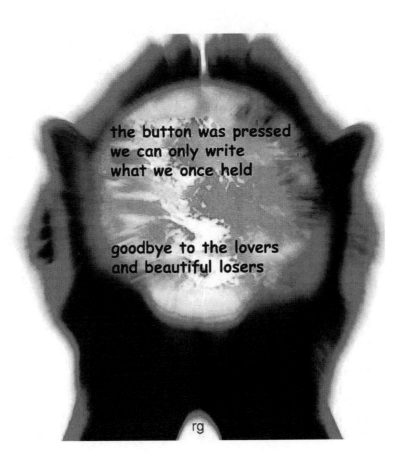

the button was pressed
we can only write
what we once held

goodbye to the lovers
and beautiful losers

rg

Air-aid

We may bomb your homes
in necessary conflict;

We may seal your borders
in necessary entrapment;

But we will send you aid
in necessary humanitarianism.

So Different

Life in his country was so different;
expected to work many hours for little reward,
no welfare state to help him through troubles
but still manages to bring up his kids without starvation
and even buy the odd treat for his wife.

He admitted to his own treats as vices;
far too much rough tobacco — three packs a week -
and, the ruination of his country, booze.
Gets hammered on Wednesdays/Thursdays
and the odd bottle on other nights too.

"I'm like a heathen praying," he laughed,
"something's somewhere - I just need to find
the bugger!" His photographs' were well fingered,
Tanya certainly seemed worth going home to
and I could see why four children quickly arrived.

We both stood, he gave an exaggerated wave,
fired a match against his new roll-up and left.
I watched the resigned burden of his walk,
primed my gun, shot him in the back.
                          I hate this bloody war.

Lower Town

The butcher isn't working today.
Taking a bus to lower town,
he's discussing distribution problems.
The conflict is affecting everyone,
no-one feels safe anymore.
The trucks have too many check-points
and are often robbed of their stock.
He's having to fetch his own, he says,
from his supplier in lower town.

The mothers are with their kids,
keeping them off school – a 'target.'
The shoppers hold resigned expressions,
forming a standing line now the seats are full.
The butcher stands for an elderly gent –
prefers to stand anyway, he says.
They talk about Israel and Palestine,
the bystander Jew and Arab.

The mothers ask what kind of world
their children will grow up in
and protectively cradle them close.
All agree that calm is needed,
that will give a chance for reason to prevail.
The butcher nods, sighs a little,
puts his hand inside his shirt.
He flips a cap with his thumb,
presses a button, shares his meat.

RAISING THE SPIRIT

"moon-silver spirals

on an evening lake".

Instant Hope

Instant hope on the hospital wall.

Celtic embroidery –

The Tree Of Life.

In India

In India, I listened.
He was yellow and gold and thirty pilgrims knelt
to absorb each word that spiralled in light.

He drew a map of my life clearly in the sand.
I understood each direction, the eventual result,
the road not taken. It was so pure, so clear.

I scooped the map into my back-pack
and carried it all my eastern journey,
physical and spiritual, until I was lost, alone.

I tipped it out onto sacred marble,
then searched the sand for the sign that read
'You Are Here.'

Releasing The Legends

The sound of my shoes on shingle,
like legends' chains to the sea;
and the wind through hands of bladderwrack
and gulls squabbling over the scree.

The silence of hawks in the still air,
my breath forming genie-lamp mist;
my mind chases free by the menhir,
cloaked angels reliving their myth.

The circle of stones that surrounds me
impregnates the air with the past,
held then by fronds of bladderwrack
until releasing the legends at last.

Eating Watermelon

The sun was already hot on Canal d'Amour.
I stirred my thick Greek coffee,
broke off my thick Greek bread.
The first small boat gnawed the sea
and water-birds shot up in a dust-bowl,
powdered nature that spiralled light
before settling on a bone dry margin plant.

The mosquito sound of a three-wheeled truck
bored its way through the morning,
stopping to throw off watermelons
before kicking up the dirt road
by the pine-and-white holiday studios
on the way to Peroulades and Sidari.

There was just the sound the morning makes,
a cicada practising for nightfall
and the spit of my seeds,
fun and squabbles for scrawny birds.
And the sea-lapped silence was lovely.
I was glad I was a writer here.
I was glad my only concern
was my pink-red watermelon slice.

St Keverne Bells

Gently through fields that are old they are calling,
St Keverne bells ring through earth's fading gold;
evening's alive with the sun as it's falling
gently through fields that are old.

Dark specks of boats in the bay of the ocean,
birthing-moon glowing and lighting their way;
St Keverne bells peal the tune to their motion –
dark specks of boats in the bay.

Those far-off lands with their faith and their teaching,
hear all God's music in heavenly ways;
St Keverne bells stretch out hands and are reaching
those far-off lands with their faith.

With prayers and sounds of love in the skyways,
St Keverne bells spread to Heaven above
and fill all life's pathways, all of life's byways,
with prayers and sounds of love.

St Keverne bells ring aloud through the nation,
cause to be happy and cause to be proud;
when the world sings in joy at His creation,
St Keverne bells ring aloud.

At Night

At night,
if you listen,
you will hear the small waves
telling the day's secrets to the
small boats.

At night,
if you listen,
you will hear the large waves
shouting the day's stories to the
large boats.

At night,
if you look hard,
you will see the ocean
wearing all of the night's stars like
jewels.

At night,
if you look hard,
you will see the ocean
sleeping on all the night's clouds like
pillows.

At night,
if you sleep hard,
you will dream of the sea
and its secrets and stories will
unfold.

Eyes Wide Open

Dance to the tune of the water on rowboat
Dance to the tune of the piper of dawn
Cry with the child who's awake in this early-day
Cry with the wild when its instincts are born

Roll with the flow of the run of the river
Roll with the goal that is driving me on
On round the bend to the break in the skyline
On through the leaves where the world is in song

Slide down the slope of the steep hill in canopy
Slide through the arches of icicle glow
Watching the seasons pass by in a smiling eye
Watching yourself in the boat down below

In The Chuska Mountains

Time stood still in the Chuska Mountains.
We were transfixed, hypnotised,
(I'm sure for a time we were floating)
looking across the cottonwoods to big sky,
clouds the size of planets, a white galaxy.
Red Rock Valley and the Carrizo Mountains
seen from high on the Buffalo Pass.

I felt a great sense of place.

You just said one word – Genesis.

Great Gable, Lake District

He poured mauve over the base green
and let it run its course.

With a white-tipped tree,
He gouged streaks and mixed pinks.

Left to dry for a million years,
He placed observers on Lingmell
and let un-roped walkers touch the sky.

Morning Lies Easy

Sunday smells
hold onto the ceiling,
like the beads
on your smile.

Lids are chattering
on the Rayburn pots,
telling us 'we're cooking'
and the morning lies easy.

Dragon's Hill (Indigo Children)

Emerging child of indigo
arising from the force
that carved the method of the man
that carved the great white horse;

the sloping grass now covers all,
the stream is slow and still,
the furrowed field disturbs the bones
that lie by Dragon's Hill.

And from these souls of indigo
the truth is holding sway;
they show the face of human race
and mankind's mind today;

their sacred semen seeds the soil
as grey-white rivers spill
to spread the gift of all who lived
and died on Dragon's Hill.

Marble Gorge

Standing on uneven rock,
your eyes are controlled by the earth's magnetism.
The browns of the near cliff dark,
the shadow thrown across to neighbouring sunlight,
where purple mountains tower,
join with blue sky, turning the river to abstract.

In the space of one footstep,
tamarisk fought for attention in the mud-sand,
limestone boulders shimmered glass
and all of the world's colours were daubed on each face,
vermillion, deepest blue,
uniting with the red and white field of mallow.

Myth of the Mountaintop Way.
I wanted the heart and soul of a Navajo,
to hear the mild breeze whisper,
honoured to see the sun spread gold on still water,
cry in Navajo wildland and sense the gods
protecting me,   destroying me.

God's Graffiti

God's graffiti;

moon-silver spirals

on an evening lake.

DIGGING UNDER THE SURFACE

"Sometimes the light that enters my head
glows far too brightly,"

St Francis In The Modern World

Just this afternoon
I ventured out with my soul
to a far lay-by
where I'd seen honeydew eyes.

I lay down gently
and stared to a higher plane,
where red shimmered to orange
in a fruit-bowl sky.

After a short while,
many of the night's creatures
called to tell of suffering,
of conflict after conflict.

I heard their stories,
I experienced their pain.
I reached to touch them
but they walked away.

A car had pulled in,
driving the innocent in fear,
leaving this prone man alone
and indolent once again.

The driver's face revealed wealth,
but poverty of purpose.
Instantly I knew - my father still had not learned.

The New Death

The crowd on the corner stared.
He held her as she turned pale,
put her hand to her throat and coughed.
'Fetch an ambulance, get a doctor!'

She slipped into unconsciousness.
The light soon glowed,
presently she shimmered,
began pulsing, strobe-like.

Sighs rose from the crowd,
some even cheered, clapped;
she was all goodness manifest.

Her hypnotic strobing caused the crowd
to blink at the same frequency.
Thus, she disappeared.

Further along, he was propped by a wall,
his skin dripping to the pavement
as her voice screamed
"What have you done?

What the hell have you done?"

Sometimes the Light

Sometimes the light that enters my head
glows far too brightly,
revealing stains and blemishes
that were once secret.

Carrying the mystic unravels mystery,
with people talking straight to the angel,
avoiding the unpleasant stare of self.

I'm bending under a dark guardian's weight,
looking for the crystal that chooses me,
searching for my own personal Jesus at the Fair.

Aborted Poem

Feeling nailed to the cross,
she was surprised not to see
blood pouring from hands and feet.

In time, living blood
stained her pure-white clothing
and poured down her cross to earth.

She pricked her finger, then slept.
In her dreams, virile men
made huge timber crosses

covered them in fine linen
and lay them at her feet,
happy with their disguise.

The wicker cot looked cosy.
She carried a package to it,
emptied something onto virgin sheets.

Walking Way Down The Country Road

singing *Pictures In The Sky*,
watching towards the white light,
going to the glow, just me,
just me and a journey of companions.

My friend the cat was struggling.
Eyelids were sewn open.
Rough stitches.
Checking sleep deprivation effects
for all of us.

He looked real tired, though.

The other cat had a shaved head.
A shaved head with a hanging wire.
Didn't ask about it.

Weather was nice, crisp winter night.
Me and a journey of companions,
right next to the shadowlands.
Dark wood.

My friend the Labrador was struggling.
Not used to walking.
Just constant swimming.
Checking muscle effects
for all of us.

He avoided the puddles, though.

The other companions were
a motley crew - mice and rabbits., rats and more dogs.
Looked like a walking hospital.
Or maybe a walking horror movie,
you know, like Mutant. Real scary.
Didn't ask about it.

Weather was nice, crisp winter night.
Out of the shadowlands
to God's shining brightness.
Well, the moon, that is.
That was the white light.
Or a neon sign.
That was the glow.
A fork in the road and a choice.

CHOOSE THE MOON!

Off went my friends.
All my journey of companions.
All my raggedy-ass-slow-walkers.
        The Fantastic Avenue they chose was

EXIT!

By a trick of light or sight
they vanished long before the horizon.
Like, they chose to die.
But they were free.

CHOOSE THE NEON!

Off I went. The Fantastic Avenue I chose was

CHRISTMAS!

Thought it looked a crisp winter night.
Along my road I saw
plenty of turkeys but heard no birdsong;
plenty of colour but saw no depth;
plenty of shops, but heard no church;
plenty of money but saw no worth.

Someone looking guilty turned away.

Someone looking innocent shouted "Happy Christmas!"
His words missed me and landed in a wine glass.
They resonated with the hollowness;
they clinked with six others in a tinsel "Cheers!"
And laughter boomed and cash tills rolled
and drunks threw up in alleyways until,
above it all,
a piercing cry.
A cry that contained all the sadness,
all the pain and terrible suffering,
all the tortured abuse of the world.
Heard by all the perpetrators,
heard by captive creatures
even when racked by electric shocks.

Someone looking guilty turned away.

A poster the size of a refuge screamed

**WE WISH A MERRY CHRISTMAS AND
A PROSPEROUS NEW YEAR.**

No-one believed it.

That was just an advertisement.

My friends,
my journey of companions,
freed in God's moonlight?
Freed from pain?
Suffering?
Their captive friends still hoping
for a present of death on Christmas morning?
God's release?
Could this be true?

I couldn't believe it.

Why should I believe it?

This is just a poem.

Seven Houses

In the First House
the freedom was pure as air
but no sign said security.
In a youthful innocence,
time spanned all summer days
as responsibility lay in margins,
the heart could beat strong rhythms
and I blew in wanton years,
seeding the wind with glorious naivety.

In the Second House
came the reality of locked doors
and the raised voices of love,
once quietly engaged, now torn.
Fear took me to wilderness,
with false safety in trees
and a tearful plea to the Sacred Heart.
I walked with a rain-clean stare
from childhood's sunlit routes.

In the Third House
open spaces were purchased for rebirth
and the rearing of values.
I could smell the future in perfumed bottles,
where houses dozed in afternoons,
my personal sun entered glades
to find me already there.
Gypsies were prepared to dance
for anyone who knew the tune.

In the Fourth House
the infinite tree of life
was encased in bind-weed magnolia
as the garden fell around me.
Dirty washing blew in public,
each hollow corner echoed faces
and white noise pulsed from the ground.
Loneliness put me on my knees
as autumn fell like sad confetti.

In the Fifth House
well-travelled bags were opened,
the blank plainness of compression eased
and laughter rang in every glass.
A tyrant was perfection of a kind
here in Bacchus' pathway,
leading to the solitary light,
leading to the solitary bed,
where reflectiveness loomed in shadows.

In the Sixth House
came the yin-yang battle,
acceptance of new belief in love
fighting grief's persistent betrayal.
Here were the signs of ancestors,
rekindling a spark from early experience
and revealing themselves in legend.
One road opened to a waste of miles,
until joined by a different direction.

In the Seventh House
the awakening spirit began to feed.
The tree blossomed into life again.
its entity accepted for its honest survival.
Beauty lay in every footfall
whether the path was muddy or dry,
with a consciousness of others' love
and hope that rose to the sky,
soaring into the sun like a phoenix.

A Walk Through The Village

Near the park swing riding with happy coloured cloth,
Nathan was holding hands with Elaine.
Small bites out of sandwiches in the picnic
and summer lying on the man, prone on the grass,
being out-snored by his grey dog.
Patrick, weathered as unsheltered stone,
walked his pathway to the sun
as the village dozed in late morning.
Funeral mourners' looked sad as the church bells tolled.
By an open window, a balloon fastened to a pram
and the raised leg of a cat's bath-time.

Perfect silence in the middle of the day.
The low rumble of a plane, its white trail trying to show me the way.
I closed my eyes.

I looked and saw
the farmer slashing grain, rooks circling for carrion.
A car left a driveway and turned
a home into a house, paper bags
into confetti for a failed marriage.
Sheep-wool was blowing on barbed wire,
Patrick watched the moor cradle the sun
and Nathan wore his love
like a hot suit on a hotter day.
Funeral mourners' flicked cigarette ash onto stones
as the church bells tolled.
By an open window, a sprinkler whirled and moaned,
a lawn spat and hissed bath-time.

Perfect silence at the end of the day.
A honey bee was dancing on my hand, trying to show me the way.
I closed my eyes.

PEOPLE ALONG THE WAY

"Their sky's so busy, so just let them keep it.
You're sky's right here and it's drawn back in secret"

Edge on Dartmoor

Edge had plonked himself down on Kings Tor,
sucking in the wilderness winds.
He'd had this wonderfully lambasted past
and now seemed happy on the granite.
He was looking the same way as us
but the dewpond ponies and patchwork
entered his eyes as the flight of dragons
entered his ears as calls from the dolmen.
He told us he saw mists inside vapours
and heard a plaintive singing from the moor's heart.

Months later he wrote and said he'd changed.
He'd been talking to a shaman, a Plains Indian,
communicating with Gaia and the Furies,
telling them about this land of permanent Hallowe'en,
eyes and sanctuary of ancient people.
I talked to old Moorhouse about him,
Moorhouse who'd lived in the high moor all his life
and who's ancestry there is some 400 years.
He didn't know about copious Orange Sunshine in sixties summers,
he just said Edge had the kind of mind that could see.
...............'even if you can't witness it - believe ....'

Visiting Felicity

Their eyes were all empty and you looked so small
squashed in the huge cushion, squashed there by the wall.

And as I looked into your pretend of night
you said "paint a picture of my flight tonight."
"Their sky's so busy, so just let them keep it.
You're sky's right here and it's drawn back in secret;
the astronaut's holding a magical sword
and weightless, cuts his umbilical cord.
He's drifting away but he knows he's alright –
millions are here on this satellite night."

You said "when I get back to the earth and sea,
paint me a picture of how it should be."

"The hospital's empty, the young nurse is yawning,
she's there to witness the birth of the morning;
the railway children by the tunnel of rain;
and the sun that bursts through instead of the train;
the black-ponied field by the white-knighted wood;
the beautiful words from the mouth of the flood;
the sheet-metal knowledge of where you belong,
you live with music, in the home of the song."

You said "that's exactly where I'm going to be,
I'm so pleased you chose to come flying with me."

Bringing it all back home
(For Johnny)

Do you remember Johnny,
the grazed-knee crawl to the railway track,
the sprawling, falling, trip coming back?
Do you remember Johnny,
when you used to hate the USA
and we thought you looked a lot like Ché?
And the smoke-filled trips to Middle Earth,
the mystic land of music and mirth,
where I was Gandalf in Rivendell
and you were Gollum moaning in hell?

Do you remember Johnny,
chemical high-times during the night,
ours filled with wonder, yours filled with fright?
We were eagle and rainbow chaser,
you were a fly - scared of newspaper.
And, sweet Kathy, I know you remember,
that first cold meet in that cold November.
And the time in the pub when she played that game,
said when you orgasm, you shout your **own** name!
She loved you, Johnny..........................
Still, we were beautiful people, Johnny, weren't we.
We were beautiful people.

Do you remember, Johnny,
the time we had in Trafalgar Square
with about a thousand people there?
We laughed as you danced to the drunken choir,
just like a spider with its arse on fire!
Then we said "I want to dance like that"
to Dylan's 'Leopard-skin Pillbox Hat'.

Anyway, Johnny, it's time to go,
Kathy'll be here next time we show.
She'll pull out the weeds, wipe your name with a tissue,
she'll smooth out your stones and she'll say we all miss you.
And we'll remember, Johnny, we'll remember,
our love through the years and tears in December.
And I'll leave behind after I've gone,
our flowers that lean towards your sun.

Indigo Nights

The pipe used with wine,
the timpany staccato,
the altered vision.
Bacchus, first seen in purple,
now cavorts in panther's skin.

Smiling decadence,
with no thought beyond tonight,
she dances for them,
music seen on flowing air,
the gypsy ballerina.

In deepest sea-blue
on primrose and taffeta,
the music loudens;
the bells of lost religion,
the bells of found fantasy.

Her clothes now spinning rainbows
over smoky air,
her circular clothes undress her
in the room's whirl,

naked, now, in indigo.

This Being Romania

After skiing, after chocolate and brandy,
I paused to watch her painting in the hallway.
It was an eagle, mirror-imaged, two-headed,
She explained the plausible tradition of it.
I explained I loved but couldn't afford it.
This being Romania, she said that was O.K.

He watched my feeble snow-plough-stop attempts
but was kind enough to say he was no better.
A day or so later we shared a sunshine beer.
He said that if he had the money, he'd ask me for books.
This being Romania, he couldn't get the classics.

The final day and a Certificate for slalom
given to all as a memento to momentum,
rented ski-boots returned for the last time.
I was approached by another familiar face;
wanted to buy my Campri - it was spare, I sold it.
This being Romania, he couldn't get this brand of jacket.

With the money, I bought the beautiful painting.
With the evening, the young man approached happily.
His mother had given him the money for his books.
He introduced me to his mother, the painter.
We laughed at the jacket-for-painting-for-books.
This being Romania, it somehow seemed so perfect.

QUITE BRIEFLY IN WALES

"our eye-path from Crickhowell to the Black Mountains, peace in the valley of the Usk."

There Was Ever a Wind off the Mountain

'There was ever a wind off the mountains'
He said that with eyes distant and love on his tongue.
I'd called up to see remnant family and friends,
re-acquaint with Welsh ale and fantastic barbed humour.
We spent all those days together,
not quite 'Last of the Summer Wine'
but enough to reconstruct the faces and buildings
in Abergavenny, the town with the big city smile.

There were some things that had not changed at all;
plastic bags were still scarecrows on the allotment;
muddy walking boots still on tarmac by hatchbacks;
sunflowers still being nosy over brick garden walls;
pub landlords chatting with vicars;
farmers with summer wellingtons;
a crowd of mourners, laughing and smoking by the gate;
and the loud crack as plastic gutters waited for water.

Cows looked content and swished their tails at flies
as we picnicked high on the slope of the Blorenge.
Everything was done in the summer's slow motion.
Sheep grew into white clouds over on the Sugar Loaf
and faint bleats blew in the valley, echoed by others out of sight
as we walked to the woods and moor of Blaenavon Top
happy that we all felt small against the striding mountains.

Days later we found old Partrishow Church,
nicely cold inside despite the day's warm breezes.
The holy rood screen, missed by Cromwell's avengers
still looked amazingly new considering its age
and, down the hill, the holy well,
where someone had placed a Bible,
messages to people and pets draped around grass palms.
You didn't have to be religious to respect this place.

The trip blew back many old memories,
the wind whipping up the rock cliffs to bird heaven,
flying half-crazed in a spiral dance above firs,
cold on my back down the clay-pebble path towards town.
Somehow, life echoes in chill air
and, here in Cornwall, my thoughts move,
back to the places and the times I'd stand high above Wales
and hear him say, *'there was ever a wind off the mountains.'*

Walking in the Forest Picture

At this hour of the evening forest
we walk in the sunlight between trees,
notice that shadows are no longer cold
and spring is now leaning towards summer.

In the stillness of the land-locked hill,
we see the field cottages below,
waiting to sleep off another day
and welcome back with orange neon.

We run down the hillside like children
pretending we're both out of control
until stopping at the stile for breath.
Back up the hill, the forest is vague,

no sound now of our crackling footsteps,
no voices where we studied moss-bark,
nothing to say we passed through like spring,
at this hour of the evening forest.

For Darren

A Girl Out Walking

When I saw her, rain was in my eyes.
She walked as if blown over grass
through many frosted pains.

On the Skirrid and Sugar Loaf hills,
the rain formed solid barriers
protecting the innocent traveller.

She was safe in the water-history,
ignorant of everything except the rainbow gulley
and the smell of mown hay.

Just outside Abergavenny,
the sun shone from the Blorenge,
burst on Blaenavon Top.

She pushed back her hood, let her hair fall.
In the freedom of familiar mists and colour,
she disappeared to the valley's comfort.

For Hannah

Quite Briefly in Wales

Quite briefly in Wales, a home at Llanover,
dogs and me walking through chanterelle wood;
Welsh border collies found the ground quite familiar,
took me to the towpath, like working dogs should.

(poems at lunchtime,
the fine Boys of Summer,
lay gold tithings barren,
hold on to each other.)

Quite briefly in Wales, a farm at Gwehelog,
the same dogs plus one in a frost-field at play;
I walked every morning, alone by self-choices,
to gather ideas for a new working day.

(cider glass, wine glass,
pipe ash just falling,
Fern Hill in vision
and verses recalling.)

Quite briefly in Wales, the garden at Gwynedd,
magnolia essence of spring in my mind;
alone, not by self-choice but sadness of circumstance,
no spirit to fight back, no spring to unwind.

(The crowd in the Angel,
words flowing like streams,
immersed in the river
to feel Dylan's dreams.)

Quite briefly in Wales, my love of a country,
quite briefly in Wales, my love of a friend;
quite briefly in Wales, my heart soared like a sun on fire,
sweet Celtic karma disguising the end.

(comfort of closeness,
late night recollection,
closeness of comfort,
our own introspection.)

The crumbling coastline, the snow on the summer beach,
moon in the seascape and village of cream;
I've laughed and I've cried and I've held on to tiny hands,
perfume and poetry, passion and dreams.
I've laughed and I've cried and I've held on to tiny hands,
quite briefly in Wales…with passion… and dreams.

In A Welsh Field

In a Welsh field with you.
We don't need the castle strongholds,
don't fear the Roman, Norman, Saxon.
We have the safety of the leaning birch,
dropping it's shadow to shade,
the comfort of the verdant green
holding bodies in warmth.

Dark in the foreground, the hedge breaks,
three firs race to the sky,
their fingers pointing to criss-cross hedges
and the dark mountain scars.
In a Welsh field with you,
watching white sky frame deepening blue,
our eye-path from Crickhowell to the Black Mountains,
peace in the valley of the Usk.

STOPPING IN SOMERSET

The honey-stoned church
Whose clock has frozen the hamlet
In stove-pipe days of sepia and gold."

Watchet Sunday

Pink, yellow and blue parade
breasting the tape to the harbour,
spreading the colours over Josephine,
over Henry's Folly, over I'm In Trouble II.

Catalogue-swarthy sailors and slick
Sunday skateboarders slide and roller
the day to pouting girls who jostle
at distance in the leaning streets

by many containered Sunday drinkers,
morose in dog-free pubs, competing
with those discussing lunch over lunch,
while watching sails waiting to sail.

Random lines of an Ancient Mariner
daubed fresh by psycho-colour graffiti
that lets us know that

*Jane and John
got it on*

beside the tree-tipped pastel hills
and three-coloured field stitched
together by hedgerows.

Watchet Sunday,
perhaps best observed
from somewhere else.

Quantocks Now

Taking now the force from a sun-driven day
We enter the Great Wood's grace and climb,
    Warned by Buzzards,
        The tree-leaf track,
    To rise above Spring-flecked slopes
Of deer-hiding Aisholt Common
And breathe new air from Somerset skies.

Turning now to gaze the Quantock Hill horizons,
Fresh with Sir Henry Newbolt eyes, and,
    Startled by Jays,
        Paint in pastels
    The honey-stoned church
Whose clock has frozen the hamlet
In stove-pipe days of sepia and gold.

Descending now to follow the Great Wood cleave,
The waymark valley of sandstone clitter where,
    Drummed by woodpeckers,
        We are content to feel small
    Against the lean of Lydeard Hill,
And, bordered by Bagborough beeches,
Watch dippers in Cockercombe Bottom's invisible stream.

Quantocks Passing

The patio daybreak sun
has seen a formation line of feathers;
among the chewed sticks and breadcrumbs,
a bird formation line on pecked grass.
These ladies-in-waiting
have competed with a four-buzzard sky
to cluck and chime in the fortunate morning.
A multi-hued wood conceals crackling bracken
on the down-slope view of churches.
Yellow-flowering gorse,
host beacon by charred acres,
showing bud trees the green way,
animal tracks the true path.
Winter, resolute in denying
access to pregnant spring, yields
to an embarrassment of greens and browns;
smouldering bark host to nature's hum
in the otherwise shimmering silence.
Shurton, Burton, Stolford,
air-linked to near fringed boundaries,
blithe tree-tipped pastel hills,
four-colour-stitched by ancient hedgerows,
and villages dusted by warm lanes.
Surface leaves are too indolent to flow,
cattle paint-stroked by red brick farms
and sheep smudged in mossed-stone shadows:
Quantocks in sunlight. Quantocks passing.

ON INTO DEVON

*"Wistman's Wood entered the mind,
darkness in a world of safety
and a hidden force in your dreams."*

Coming To Dartmoor

Maybe you'll come when the hazel catkins
wave the promise of autumn fruit,
or heavy frost is melted by sun
turning meadow-grass to bright chandeliers.

Maybe you'll come when the bluebells and purple orchids
lead to new primroses by the wood
and hawthorn-scented air rises above the pink
of bell-heather and western gorse.

Maybe you'll come when the pearl fritillary
blows to the wild violets,
or larval clover gives birth to common blue,
opening its page-wings to green alkanet.

Maybe you'll avoid the boggy ground
where forget-me-nots thrive beside moorland streams,
yellow asphodel and St John's Wort form bright towers
and cotton-grass heads wait to fly.

Maybe you'll resist running wild with ponies,
shouting loud from granite tors,
circling with windless, weightless buzzards
and be happily unknown in the wilderness.

Maybe you'll leave in a foxglove-summer,
carrying its memory in the heart and stars,
or when heathers' perfume lies on the warm days drift
and the unicorns gather to graze......

Over Longash Hill

The stunted hawthorn,
strong by the standing copse,
time-leans in the face of swaying wood-sorrel
and moor-grass dances in continuous wind.

The mirror-brook,
reflecting the rush fantasy,
coats the avenues of fallen dolmen, hill sanctuary
in the ages of Black Death.

The open sky
holds the skylark's circle
and frames a horizon of history,
a time-capsule achievement of washed stone.

Free Dawn on the Mystic Moor

Birdsong in this bracken-oak
And golden on the distant tor,
Peeling back the velvet cloak,
Free dawn on the mystic moor.
The new-soaked, dew-soaked, mystic moor.

Silver lingers coiled around
The ancient whispers in the woods
And in the carpet-moss abounds
The toadstools sheltered under hoods.
Tree-borne, free dawn, whispered woods.

Dog-fox darting out to greet it,
Glistening droplets of angel-bright,
Penetrating darkness underneath it,
Dancing bowls of freefall light
Earth-fed, birth-red, freefall light.

Timeless now, the sweetest water,
Just as she had laughed at moonshine,
Rises up through granite's falter
To say hello and laugh at sunshine.
Sweetest, deepest, laugh at sunshine.

Past the still and slumbering oaks,
Spitting her spray at vixen yawning,
She hurries on past Gandalf's folk
And clicks the keys to the Dartmoor morning.
Spray-making, day-breaking, free dawn morning.

So leave the weeping of mankind
And follow me from moor to sea
Here there is a soul to find,
Join the dawn and join it free.
Golden on the distant tor,
Free dawn on the mystic moor.

Wistman's Wood Revisited

The veil between two worlds was thin,
its position in storm torture,
a labyrinth of stunted oaks.
This gothic world revealed to us
in sylvan archaeology.
Forces called to the primeval,
where leaves searched vainly for sunlight
in the land of darkness and held
aroma from lost centuries.

New life twisted to the heavens,
its roots in decayed, deformed branch.
Beard fungus of the lightest green
in excessive humidity.
Polypody and epiphytes,
a touch like velvet on mossed bark.
Whortleberries and coral moss
fighting always for life forces,
holding firm in the purest air.

The fledgling Dart played its music,
a common lizard shone in sunlight.
The distant sound of grasshoppers
and water by the waiting hill
met the heavy-grazing Galloways
as they kept watch over this ancient home.
Wistman's Wood entered the mind,
darkness in a world of safety
and a hidden force in your dreams.

Dartmoor Regression

In a midnight symphony of colour,

high ravens' wings

rustling at

weather's

edge.

Eyes

with tales,

pale moon hands

stroke standing stones

giving a glimpse of earth's pre-history.

Incident

Just off the Whitchurch Road
where the moor starts on the downs,
he rolled a Rizla with practised perfection.

The lady with the border terriers
told him he was much too young;
he told her she was a nosy cow.

Where the established gorse
ran to the bordering wood,
he heard a small bird cheeping.

He tried to feed it grass,
then dropped a rock on it.
Just like his, the parents were nowhere.

Buzzards over Dartmoor

Where Pork Hill levelled a little,
we hung a left by the ponies,
standing in the shade by the dewpond.
It was hot by the soft grasses,
hotter still in the Cox Tor valley.
You led the way in denim shorts,
I followed, all bare-chest bustle,
right to the top of high Roos Tor
for a picnic in the heavens.

The heat was shadowing far mist,
no sign of the sky collapsing.
With our backs on flatter granite
we watched four buzzards in free flight.
No visible movement of air,
riding the high roller-coaster,
pulled like puppets on string,
hidden by the faintest outline of clouds.
Even when quite close, no sound
to call attention to the dance.

Finally, with a faint dip of wings,
they found a new valley. Gone.
Walking back, the coloured moor deserted,
sheep in the shade of boulders,
we had wishes given as children -
we both wished our feet were talons,
we both wished our arms were strong wings.

Tavy Cleave

The Tavy River, open arms of welcome for lost disciples;
Rattlebrook, Kneeset, Cuthill and Fur Tor,
grateful for this accessed escape, pouring waters
to join the steep, rocky, onward journey.

The murmuring sound of Tavy Cleave,
whispering secrets to fern and bathing rock,
bouncing the starburst of sunlight
to Narcissus' constant mirror-image.

Nature is singing in resonance to the heather,
held in the curved spine of Western Gorse
and roaring a warning to soft, waving rush,
to frosted Hazel Catkins.

The deep gorge is in choir union,
the mist-cymbal of celestial ammil,
ice-orchestra playing to the wild,
amplified by granite battlements.

The sound reduces to the river flow,
now easing through resting Tavistock,
to the path of the conquering Tamar,
with its song of the seasons unending.

*ammil – where each blade of grass, each leaf,
is frozen and the slightest breeze brings a tinkling
like wind-chimes in the silent air*

Western Face

Take my map and follow the ink-marks.
I hope you hit Great Mis Tor on a clear day,
when the clouds float stepping-stones on Walkham Valley
and you are carried behind Cocks Hill,
unprepared for the might and thunder of Tavy Cleave.

I hope you can find my soul by the old wall,
see my memory climbing far Ger Tor
and follow my last hope on high Great Links.
To find me, just follow the ink-marks.
They lead to spiritual fulfilment,
out there on the Western Face.

By Devonport Leat

Another long spring day.
The sky was tinged purple as we crossed the flat moor,
the wind carrying drift of a lone curlew's cry.
Devonport Leat in haze, rolling to Burrator.

We passed the Foxtor Mires, remembering stories,
deaths and narrow escapes. Royal Hill before us,
Whiteworks, where tin was mined,
industry in the wild.

Now upon the long ridge by Hameldown's skyline
we rested and listened to the breeze at Bellever,
a cushioned sound of trees, a reminder of the force
that lay waiting, resting.

On over the whiteness to Rippon Tor's welcome,
before the Devon lane snaked homeward just for us
and Devonport Leat yawned onward in the sun.

On Crockern Tor

Whatever we'd intended just didn't matter.
Locked together on Crockern Tor,
the summer valley breaking its beauty
as we breathed in moorland air
and saw dreams over the hill
coming true just for us.

Inquisitive sheep gathered safe in their distance,
watching us share their world
and lazy clouds drifted,
the birthing Dart reflecting deepest blue
as scents of summer colour
surrounded us there.

Galloways rested in the summer haze,
skirting the stretched green-black wood.
Volumes of silence bound love's memories
as the day's picture framed under cushioning sky.
Echoes remind me now how much I love there.
Crockern Tor is waiting with a new sweet song.

Moonfall Venford Reservoir

You came to Dartmoor for just
a few days' break.
We decided late to stroll along
past the hedge, an under-used path
guiding us to the moor's heart.
Soon, a pale moon-glow shone
to a margin of stars, Ryder Hill behind,
Venford Reservoir ahead.

We stood by the trees, shadowed
in autumn undress.
At the water's edge we
looked to night's hidden shades,
indigo brushstrokes
and spirals of moon-silver,
a moving landscape
to be viewed in pure silence,
sky and air gentle
in delicate translucence.

It seemed to us then
that to make the slightest sound
would startle nature
and this vision disappear
like a frightened fox.

We left with peaceful footsteps,
autumn's curtain drawn,
a lullaby of breeze for
cradled night creatures.
Moonfall, Venford Reservoir.

RESTING IN CORNWALL

*"where Helford's cottages hide in looming trees
and mists rise clear above still masts."*

My Breeze

My breeze sweeps off the sea into Coverack,
where it meets the Moho and cleanses the tides;
where it ruffles the legs of oystercatchers,
cries in song with the curlew, lifts the buzzard.

My breeze warms the air for daffodil and orchid,
takes the Peacock and Copper to spring quill;
seeds the air with valerian and campion,
rocks the ox-eye daisies on wilderness cliffs.

My breeze carries the ancient cry of the vixen
across the co-axial fields of Lowland Point,
raising the heads of Neolithic workers,
the Romano-Cornish gathering furze for fires.

My breeze blows gossamer to evening waves,
hastens the freshwater through Godrevy reed-beds;
it spirals in the past centuries of St. Keverne
and whispers the names of long-dead mariners.

My breeze fades in the sepia tints of dawn,
where shadows mirror flat on the river;
where Helford's cottages hide in looming trees
and mists rise clear above still masts.

My breeze takes me to wild Goonhilly Downs,
to the rambling estates and country houses;
to coves and meadowland, serpentine and winter beaches;
to the heart that beats forever in Cornwall.

Moho — where the earth's mantle meets the oceanic crust

Portloe

Paint green spines, then blur with black
across the left-hand corner to frame;

sweep the centre with browns,
fade sky-blue horizon to turquoise and indigo;

place white squares randomly by a sand-coloured slope;
fill the frame with sweeps of silver,
highlighted in reflective mauves.

You now have a headland, a sandy cove,
white cottages tumbling to the sea,
the calm sea on a calm day.

Don't be tempted to change a thing.

Let it come to life.

Catchin' Up His Heels

Billy Bray the Cornish miner
fought and swore through life,
stole the family savings,
drank the family money.

People said Billy'd been to hell
they said his words 'smelt o' sulphur.'
Then Billy Bray fought the bible;
then Billy Bray lost to the hymnbook.

He voiced evangelism loud
through the roads and rugged fields,
his voice both pure and awful,
the nightingale and the raven.

He danced days in an upsurge wind,
'catchin' up his heels,' leading the thousands
in a hundred miles of voice
through the lanes and the rolling downs.

Seasons on Coverack Lane

The storm clouds were shaded greys
but from somewhere the land glowed,
stone walls, bare trees and single track,
all with rustic gold, delicate shadows.

Hardy snow held on to the verge-side gulleys.
It was silent. It was naked and vulnerable.
The trees lifted the weight of winter
and a silver face shone on the beeches.

Fires were being extinguished, lungs renewed
as buds hid their early bodies,
waiting for the last battles to end,
the killing frost, the wind's roaring lion.

The lane's centre now invaded with green,
testimonial tyre-tracks by the grasses,
the dense silence of ferns holding all.
The air is heavy again, cumulus builds.

All sky is cotton-towered.
The storm breaks.
Earth turns its stomach to welcome rain.

Helford Dawn. Summertime.

This illuminated land shines a picture,
a high-wheeling buzzard in morning glory.
Darkened skyline trees form green coats
and sky is drawn back for day.

The pre-milk herd cast shadows,
copy-cat in a silhouetted formation line,
while the mist melts in expectant glare –
the musical birth of the sun.

Helford dawn. Summertime.

And On A Springtime Night

No sound of traffic and on a springtime night,
Killigrew Street to the pound of the pier;
a Falmouth horizon, a harbour-view sight;
reflections on water and shapes drawing near.

Murmur of people and on a springtime night,
see Kilnquay Wood to the point at Trefusis;
boy makes an offer to a girl at his side -
she laughs, she thinks, in the end she refuses.

These two had been through much stormier weather
on this tee-shirt night over black combat jeans;
Zippo a roll-up, then walk off together,
he says what he meant but she knows what he means.

Sun dies in the water, the sea turns slate-black
and the last ferry-boat comes home from St Mawes;
take a last breath of sky before we turn back
from harbour and sea, through the town without doors.

The closing of day and on a springtime night,
we face evening's sea breezes by Fish Strand Quay;
watch moon on the water play tricks with the light,
with thoughts of tomorrow, a lady and me.

The Man In The Hedge

The man in the hedge served Sir William.
Found in the deep midwinter,
half-savage, gentle simpleton.

He would guard Sir William all night,
run with his horse, gentle as a spaniel.
At Sir William's request he would eat nettles,

live birds and fishes, burning coals.
He slept face-down, heels-up,
away from the glares of the day.

When his strength became less,
he was once more abandoned to survive.
He crossed all manner of country

until he found his hedge again.
He lay there until death discovered him,
found in the deep midwinter.

Seagulls over Coverack

I thought she was doing homework
her dictionary being rifled with menace..
Flashing furrowed-brow black looks
when my singing disturbed thought,
channelling its way from beneath blond hair
to the exposed tongue, held firmly by teeth.

'If it's too hard, I'll help,' I'd volunteered,
but my attempts were dutifully ignored,
unlike Tuesday's maths which clashed with television
and left me fulfilled that $X = 4.75$ metres.
Finally, hands on hips by the settled fire,
she watched her thrown offerings burn,
poking each charred scrap until just ash
and kissing me goodnight without customary cuddle,
all her failed attempts obviously being my fault.

I looked at the screwed-up paper balls
hurled with increasing strength into wicker.
Four unravelled pieces of lined paper,
each starting 'Seagulls over Coverack,'
then petering out with scribbles and one swear word.

"She's been trying to write you a poem," you said;
and with the image and sound of that one written line,
'Seagulls over Coverack'…she had.

Afternoon Hotel

Decanted from a wine-coloured coach,
they poured noisily into the lounge.
A fine time in studied green waistcoats,
the manner of money over reality,
some settled in ornate wood,
others in chequered splendour.

Pink and gingham, beige and stripe
pushed metal into meat and veg.
The pint poured power and the gin-and-it smiled.
Flowing babble over red cabbage and ragout
interspersed with Vogue and Capote,
the quiet couple heavening over fruit and brandy wafer.

A bell clanged cream-tea Cornwall
and gave business a smile and routine,
comfort found in a cashmere'd way.
The horse-lady grated with her 'competition stride'
and an adjacent four heads joined in centre table –
'always one show-off,' the mutual whisper, 'always one.'

'Sorry to leave,' said some, 'do it again soon.'
Yes, maybe on a sunny day of gossip
or at the edge of weather with love.
Black-and-white waitresses descended like gulls,
removing all traces, collecting the coins.
Afternoon hotel, somewhere south-west.

Goonhilly Downs In The Mist

Goonhilly Downs in the mist
and indistinct voices sing settlement,
a mock cloud runs over heather
and gorse towers to leaning trees.

No sheep to forage in grey,
no lined ponies or all-leg foals
to drink from the sweet-water trough,
no distant children's echo.

Cars reveal the eyes of night foxes
snaking the bushes of lane,
running hollow on thunder grass
to their peaceful sleep in the light.

Another Lizard Dawn

The first light had drowned the wind.
The puppet sun had been pulled from its shadow canopy
and it scorched the Lizard mist.

Soft night had already died
and doors opened deep into souls, naked in dewpond hills,
whispered in gossiping streams.

The sun held hard in focus,
lighting each path, each church, in a pattern of seeded air,
echoes and distant movement.

Day complete, night was ready
for blind stars to chase the camera memories of dusk
and shine over cooling coves.

The moon's face was ruling now,
painting the same brushstrokes that caused us to rise, newly born,
in another Lizard dawn.

Indigo Dreams Publishing
132 Hinckley Road
Stoney Stanton
Leicestershire
LE9 4LN
UK
www.indigodreams.co.uk